The NFL's Greatest Teams

JACKSONVILLE JAGUARS

Katie Lajiness

Big Buddy Books
An Imprint of Abdo Publishing
abdopublishing.com

abdopublishing.com

Published by Abdo Publishing, a division of ABDO, PO Box 398166, Minneapolis, Minnesota 55439.

Printed in the United States of America, North Mankato, Minnesota.
092016
012017

THIS BOOK CONTAINS RECYCLED MATERIALS

Cover Photo: ASSOCIATED PRESS.
Interior Photos: ASSOCIATED PRESS.

Coordinating Series Editor: Tamara L. Britton
Graphic Design: Michelle Labatt, Taylor Higgins, Jenny Christensen

Publisher's Cataloging-in-Publication Data

Names: Lajiness, Katie, author.
Title: Jacksonville Jaguars / by Katie Lajiness.
Description: Minneapolis, MN : Abdo Publishing, 2017. | Series: NFL's greatest teams | Includes bibliographical references and index.
Identifiers: LCCN 2016944877 | ISBN 9781680785357 (lib. bdg.) | ISBN 9781680798951 (ebook)
Subjects: LCSH: Jacksonville Jaguars (Football team)--History--Juvenile literature.
Classification: DDC 796.332--dc23
LC record available at http://lccn.loc.gov/2016944877

Contents

A Winning Team 4
League Play 6
Kicking Off 8
Highlight Reel 10
Halftime! Stat Break 14
Coaches' Corner 16
Star Players 18
EverBank Field 22
Go Jaguars! 24
Final Call 26
Through the Years 28
Postgame Recap 30
Glossary 31
Websites 31
Index 32

A Winning Team

The Jacksonville Jaguars are a football team from Jacksonville, Florida. They have played in the National Football League (NFL) for more than 20 years.

The Jaguars have had good seasons and bad. But time and again, they've proven themselves. Let's see what makes the Jaguars one of the NFL's greatest teams.

Teal, black, gold, and white are the team's colors.

71 TONY BOSELLI
PRIDE OF THE JAGUARS

League Play

Team Standings

The AFC and the National Football Conference (NFC) make up the NFL. Each conference has a north, south, east, and west division.

The NFL got its start in 1920. Its teams have changed over the years. Today, there are 32 teams. They make up two conferences and eight divisions.

The Jaguars play in the South Division of the American Football Conference (AFC). This division also includes the Houston Texans, the Indianapolis Colts, and the Tennessee Titans.

The Tennessee Titans are a major rival of the Jaguars.

Fans get excited to watch the Jaguars play!

Kicking Off

In 1989, the Touchdown Jacksonville! group wanted to bring an NFL team to the city. By 1992, Jacksonville was one of five cities in the running. The next year, the NFL picked the Jacksonville Jaguars to join the league!

In 2012, team owners Wayne and Delores Weaver were honored by the Jaguars. The Weavers owned the team for 18 years.

Highlight Reel

The Jaguars started play in 1995. More than 70,000 fans filled the stadium to see their first home game.

In 1996, the Jaguars had their first winning season. They made it to the play-offs! The Jaguars won their division by beating the Denver Broncos 30–27! Sadly, the team lost the AFC title game to the New England Patriots 20–6.

Win or Go Home

NFL teams play 16 regular season games each year. The teams with the best records are part of the play-off games. Play-off winners move on to the conference championships. Then, conference winners face off in the Super Bowl!

In 1995, Mark Brunell was the first player to be traded to the Jaguars.

In 1997, Jimmy Smith celebrated after catching a 16-yard touchdown in the divisional play-off game.

The Jaguars made it to the play-offs for the next three seasons. In 2000, the Jaguars won the divisional title again. But, they lost to the Tennessee Titans in the conference **championship**.

In 2002, the Jaguars moved from the AFC Central Division to the South Division. The team struggled to have winning seasons. Today, the Jaguars are working hard to improve.

The Jaguars played the New York Jets in the 1999 play-offs. Running back Fred Taylor (28) rushed 135 yards and scored one touchdown!

Still Waiting

As of 2016, the Jaguars are one of four NFL teams to never have played in a Super Bowl.

Rashean Mathis made two interceptions during the wildcard play-off game in 2008.

Halftime! Stat Break

Team Records

RUSHING YARDS
Career: Fred Taylor, 11,271 yards (1998–2008)
Single Season: Maurice Jones-Drew, 1,606 yards (2011)

PASSING YARDS
Career: Mark Brunell, 25,698 yards (1995–2003)
Single Season: Blake Bortles, 4,428 yards (2015)

RECEPTIONS
Career: Jimmy Smith, 862 receptions (1995–2005)
Single Season: Jimmy Smith, 116 receptions (1999)

ALL-TIME LEADING SCORER
Josh Scobee, 1,022 points (2004–2014)

Famous Coaches

Tom Coughlin (1995–2002)
Jack Del Rio (2003–2011)

Championships

SUPER BOWL APPEARANCES:
None

SUPER BOWL WINS:
None

Pro Football Hall of Famers & Their Years with the Jaguars

None

Fan Fun

STADIUM: EverBank Field
LOCATION: Jacksonville, Florida
MASCOT: Jaxson De Ville

Coaches' Corner

Tom Coughlin was the team's first head coach. He led the Jaguars to four straight play-offs. During his eight years with the team, Coughlin had a 68–60 regular-season record.

In 2003, Jack Del Rio became the team's second head coach. That year, he helped the defense improve to second best in the NFL. He led the team to two play-offs in nine years.

Gus Bradley became head coach in 2013.

In 1996, Coughlin led the Jaguars to the AFC championship game.

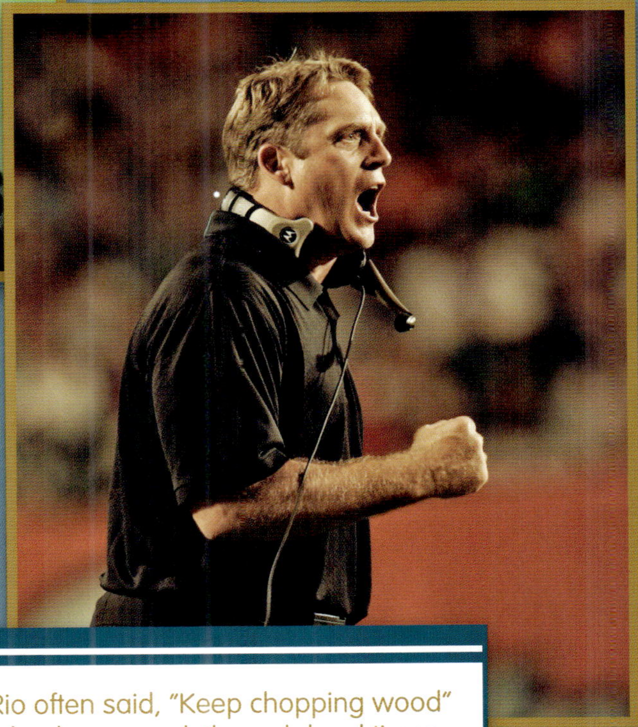

Del Rio often said, "Keep chopping wood" to help players work through hard times.

Star Players

Tony Boselli OFFENSIVE TACKLE (1995–2001)

In 1995, Tony Boselli was the Jaguars' first-ever **draft** pick. At 6'7" (2 m) and 322 pounds (146 kg), he was a strong force on the team's offensive line. In 2006, Boselli became the first player named into the Pride of the Jaguars, which is the team's hall of fame.

Mark Brunell QUARTERBACK (1995–2003)

Mark Brunell joined the team in 1995. During his **career** with the Jaguars, he completed 2,184 passes and threw for 144 touchdowns. These are both team records! Brunell was invited to play in the Pro Bowl, which is the NFL's all-star game, three times.

Jimmy Smith WIDE RECEIVER (1995–2005)

Jimmy Smith almost had to quit the NFL due to illness. But, the Jaguars signed him in 1995. Many consider Smith to be the best receiver in the team's history! He holds the team record for most receptions, receiving yards, and touchdown catches.

Fred Taylor RUNNING BACK (1998–2008)

Fred Taylor was the ninth-overall pick in the 1998 **draft**. As a **rookie**, he rushed for 1,223 yards and 14 touchdowns. In 2000, Taylor made a 90-yard touchdown run during a play-off game. That set an NFL record! During his 11 years with the team, he had seven 1,000-yard seasons.

Rashean Mathis CORNERBACK (2003–2012)

The Jaguars picked Rashean Mathis in the 2003 draft! Mathis helped the Jaguars beat the Pittsburgh Steelers in the 2008 play-offs. In that game, he had two **interceptions**, returning for one touchdown. His team records include 30 **career** interceptions and 512 interception return yards.

Maurice Jones-Drew RUNNING BACK (2006–2013)

Maurice Jones-Drew spent eight years with the Jaguars. During that time, the Jaguars had only one winning season. But, that didn't stop Jones-Drew from working hard. In 2011, he rushed for 1,606 yards and set a team record! He also holds a team record with 81 total touchdowns.

Blake Bortles QUARTERBACK (2014–)

The Jaguars picked Blake Bortles third in the 2014 **draft**. In 2015, he set many team records. Bortles threw for five touchdowns in a single game. He had 15 straight games with a passing touchdown. And, he had the most single-season passing touchdowns and passing yards.

EverBank Field

The Jaguars play home games at EverBank Field. It is in Jacksonville. EverBank Field opened in 1995. It holds about 67,000 people.

EverBank Field was host to the 2005 Super Bowl.

EverBank Field can expand to hold more than 82,000 fans for events such as the Super Bowl.

Go Jaguars!

Thousands of fans flock to EverBank Field to see the Jaguars play home games.

The team's **mascot** is Jaxson De Ville. He helps fans cheer on their team at home games.

Jaxon De Ville ziplines onto the field during home games!

Final Call

The Jaguars have a long, rich history. Over the years, they made six play-off appearances. They won their division title twice.

Even during losing seasons, true fans have stuck by them. Many believe the Jacksonville Jaguars will remain one of the greatest teams in the NFL.

In 2015, the Jaguars and the Buffalo Bills played at Wembley Stadium in London, England.

Through the Years

1993

The Jaguars are founded by a group called Touchdown Jacksonville!

1995

The Jaguars begin play in the NFL.

1997

Quarterback Mark Brunell is named Pro Bowl Most Valuable Player (MVP).

2000

Fred Taylor sets a team record by rushing 234 yards in one game.

2003

Jack Del Rio becomes the new head coach.

2006

The Jaguars introduce a team hall of fame called Pride of the Jaguars.

2008

The Jaguars beat the Philadelphia Eagles 31–29 in the play-offs.

2012

Shahid Khan becomes the new owner of the team.

Postgame Recap

1. Who is the team's mascot?
   A. K.C. Wolf **B.** Jaxson De Ville **C.** Roary

2. What is the name of the stadium where the Jaguars play home games?
   A. Sally Field
   B. CenturyLink Field
   C. EverBank Field

3. What year did the Jaguars play their first game?
   A. 1995
   B. 1996
   C. 1997

4. How many Jaguars players are in the Pro Football Hall of Fame?
   A. 0
   B. 5
   C. 13

1. B. 2. C. 3. A. 4. A.

Glossary

career a period of time spent in a certain job.

championship a game, a match, or a race held to find a first-place winner.

draft a system for professional sports teams to choose new players.

interception (ihn-tuhr-SEHP-shuhn) when a player catches a pass that was meant for the other team's player.

mascot something to bring good luck and help cheer on a team.

rookie a first-year player in a professional sport.

Websites

To learn more about the NFL's Greatest Teams, visit **booklinks.abdopublishing.com**. These links are routinely monitored and updated to provide the most current information available.

Index

Alltel Stadium **22**
American Football Conference **6, 10, 11, 12, 17**
Bortles, Blake **14, 21**
Boselli, Tony **18**
Bradley, Gus **16**
Brunell, Mark **11, 14, 19, 28**
Buffalo Bills **27**
Central Division **12**
Coughlin, Tom **14, 16, 17**
Del Rio, Jack **14, 16, 17, 29**
Denver Broncos **10**
England **27**
EverBank Field **10, 15, 22, 23, 24**
fans **7, 10, 24, 26**
Florida **4, 8, 15, 22**
Houston Texans **6**
Indianapolis Colts **6**
Jones-Drew, Maurice **14, 21**
Khan, Shahid **29**
mascot **15**
Mathis, Rashean **13, 20**
National Football Conference **6**
National Football League **4, 6, 8, 10, 13, 16, 19, 20, 26, 28**
New England Patriots **10**
New York Jets **13**
Philadelphia Eagles **29**
Pittsburgh Steelers **20**
play-offs **10, 12, 13, 16, 20, 26, 29**
Pro Bowl **19, 28**
Pro Football Hall of Fame **15**
Smith, Jimmy **11, 14, 19**
South Division **6, 10, 11, 12, 26**
Super Bowl **10, 13, 14, 22, 23**
Taylor, Fred **13, 14, 20, 28**
Tennessee Titans **6, 7, 12**
Touchdown Jacksonville! **8, 28**
Weaver, Delores **9**
Weaver, Wayne **9**
Wembley Stadium **27**